Pink Geishas and OtherPoems

BY

Mary F. Tomaselli

ISBN: 0-75963-215-4

This book is printed on acid free paper.

1stBooks - rev. 4/23/01

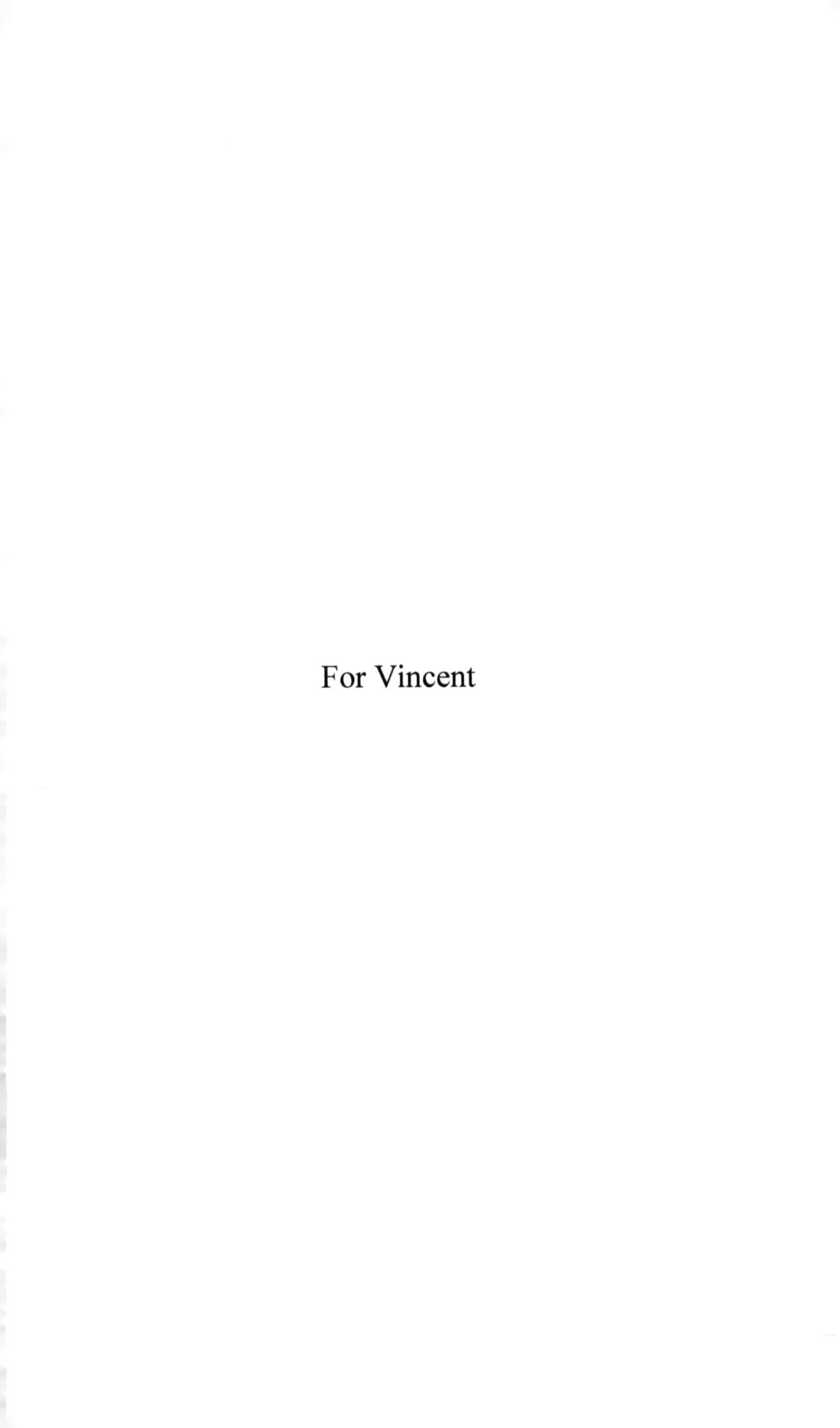

For Vincent

Pink Geishas

There is a time in winter,
in late afternoon,
when the sun shines intensely pink
through stained glass,
and fills the room with a glow,
infusing small alabaster figures
on the mahogany side table
with a pale pink light.

The delicate geishas,
from ancient Shogun days,
in perpetual pause on their stage,
play their venerable instruments:
pipes, flute and samisen —

And then I can hear it, oh yes I can:
the fragile strains of an Asian melody,
assuaging my ear
too long used to Western sounds.

ALL THE MEN & HORSES

At the hotel in Siena, the note said,
"Vincent called," so I called you,
and you said, "happy birthday early."

The door to the street has the pattern of a mosaic
but it's not, more like a Seurat by someone with fat fingers
who must be color blind, but is probably making a living at it,
and that's more than I can say about real artists.
In the morning, the city smells of marble, wine and fertilizer,
which reminds me of that great opening scene in *Much Ado,*
where all the men & horses are galloping right at you and kicking up dirt,
making your heart and some other parts of your body throb
because you know why they're in such a hurry to get home.
I wish you had said I love you or something.
The *duomo* looks like every other cathedral I've seen,
a redundant reminder that God lives in heaven
and everybody cares enough to go without,
and put their hard-earned money in the basket.
I want to stop for something cold
but I'll be damned if I'll pay 5000 lire for warm Coke.

Going on Nerve, or Talking to Frank O'Hara

Frank,
I've read almost all of your work in the last 3 days,
and the tears still hang around my eyes.
Only a short while ago, I had never heard of you.
When another poet said your name,
I read you, and now I don't recognize myself or my poetry.
My poems are heavy, plodding, profound in the worst way,
yours are right there —"beautiful lies."
I hold back and you run toward,
I explain and pontificate you sweat the details,
I describe the moonlight, you talk to the Sun.

But, Frank, my poetry is becoming

BACKYARD

Clothespinned and flipped over, Picasso's lovers, one-eyed, embracing, hangs upside-down above tomatoes, basil and white lilies. Would he be happy to see how far he's come?

EMBRACE

The coming together of arms
as in a war, embracement on battlements,
or family reunions, bumping old battle-axes.
Something like the rapist's stranglehold,
closer to Saran smothering peas or the deadly embrace.
If not, then blood coagulating on white sheets
that billow at the window the day after consummation.
As, years later, jeans hug hips in quiet desperation.
Unlike the hold up at the corner deli
or the job of clothespins.
Just like the Christian born again, and again embracing faith,
or my wish for my mother's

Mary F. Tomaselli

EMERGENCY ROOM

White coat whispers condolences
to black & white bridegroom,
while crooked duck-billed cane leans in a corner,
and pregnant woman sets off Geiger counter
and Rostafarian knits table-mats.
Child vomiting directions on the wall,
Koreans lost in *General Hospital.*
"Will someone please answer that phone?"
Woman in orange awning watches ambulances through blind slats,
patient Washington to registration.
Corrupted chap from Cheltenham paces in straight lines
and commercial jingles dance on the ceiling.
Washed-up counselor lays wounded camper across chairs,
fit occasion for reading "Patient's Bill of Rights"
and Morris of the duck-billed cane complains greedily
about his crazy whippet of a wife.
"Will someone pu...lease answer that goddamned phone?!"

GREEK THEATRE

the bad end unhappily, the good unluckily. That is what tragedy means —

Tom Stoppard

Dionysus watches from the dancing circle
the chorus chants and dances,
opening scene with recitative,
saffron robes trailing.
The Hero in his mask, grotesque, elongated
(the gods know who he is)
presumes to walk the crimson tapestries
(red carpet to you),
and will pay for the transgress— we know it—tearing out his beard,
plucking out his eyes,
the Messenger has prophesied it.

Don't we know it? or wish it?
"She's gonna pay" "He'll get his"
"What goes around comes around"—
prophecy with a vengeance.

But the drama of it is, and the truth,
is that Fate is a cruel character,
and heaven is not up there in the rafters
or even waiting in the wings.
Sacrifice is no respecter of fatal flaws.
Cassandra of the haunted eyes
has nothing to say to us that we don't already know.

HAIKU

Woman sits
with swaddled, battered knee,
reading and healing

Late summer rain —
fringe of feathery marigolds
soaked and bowed

We returned from lunch
he kissed my lips lightly —
he has my heart

DOGWOOD

When I was little
somebody told me
that Christ was crucified
on a limb of the dogwood tree.
And that ever after,
the dogwood flower grew
in the shape of a cross
and was stained red on the tips
with His blood.
Now, whenever I see that tree
I think of that.

Black Bear

(from a news item)

How did you get here,
in a park in Queens?
Your guts exposed to the world,
hair matted with congealed blood.
Was it some crazy cult ritual,
or a terribly inept hunter?
Did you leave little ones alone & hungry?
Ah, but you can’t worry about that now.

Stars

Wear the stars for a necklace,
18 inches or 24.
Wear a black dress,
stars look their best against a dark background.
Show them off for the evening,
You'll have to give them back in the morning

JULY 4TH AT ROBERT MOSES STATE PARK

You smell it before you see it,
scrub pine, sea, salt air.
Long finger of seacoast
preserved by Mr. Moses.
We are all grateful.
Gulls swoop toward protected dunes,
footsteps sink in the morning gloom,
pale green, wave-bound sea sometimes,
calm and rippling today, but cold.
Coffee in white cups,
worshippers turning faces up to the sun.
Gulls gather against a blue sky
hoping for scraps of breakfast bread tossed away.
Bikinis made of stars & stripes
undulate along the foamy edge.
Turtles in their nesting places
wait for the end to the faces at steering wheels,
and the return of peace & quiet.

EBOLA

(reports from Kinshasa, Zaire, May 18-31, 1995)

The fugitives of Kikwit are trapped,
The quarantine has been ordered,
The roadblock is up,
Because the capital must be saved.

No matter that they cry and plead for mercy,
No matter that the nuns are dying,
"They cannot come in," the governor says,
"They cannot come in -
and they must not touch the corpses."
It's important - the virus kills 9 out of 10,
but they must not touch the corpses.

The governor and the minister will meet on Thursday,
"We need a plan of action."
But the fugitives of Kikwit are bleeding
And another nun is dying.

The governor says,
"The fever can't reach here, millions of people will die.
The city can accommodate 150 corpses,
just 150 corpses..."

But the fugitives of Kikwit are dying,
And the road is strewn with corpses.

The Elephants Are Weeping...

Blood is coloring the river,
a sign of the epidemic run free,
monkeys make a sound like keening,
because Gaspar is dead in the grass.

He was the first infected by Ebola,
he was a friend of the animals they say,
he brought the fever to the village without knowing,
and now he is dead in the grass.

There is no one to bury his body,
no one to mourn and remember.
They're all fleeing the village,
they've left Gaspar alone in the grass.

The elephants gather, they are weeping,
The tigers moan deep in their grief,
they are the only ones left to mark his passing,
Gaspar who died in the grass.

GREETINGS

I never liked you.
you, in your whiny, self-centered way,
have annoyed me these 40 years.
I don't care that you're old now,
and frail and white-haired.

Your daughter has always loved you,
and you, you have wheedled,
and whined, instilling in her a fear of living,
loving, and trying new things.
You have always been a small woman.

I take up my pen today
because it is your 90th birthday
and I wanted to write something appropriate:
"Happy Birthday.
I wonder why God let you live so long?"

Mary F. Tomaselli

Mohonk Mountain House

(Haiku)

The road is long and winding
pines, birches above -
"Slowly and Quietly Please"

The mountain house rises,
stone gazebo standing sentry—
weeping beech drapes the road

Rock faces rising to Skytop
rough wood gazebos here and there—
early sun sets the lake shining

Swallows circling the bell-less belfry—
canoes like dead carcasses
come alive when the sun climbs higher

Apple blossom tree
like a wedding bower—
shelters a stone bench

Sun coaxes ferns to uncurl
in the rock garden...
hummingbirds!

Rocking chairs
like soldiers at attention...
cardinals clicking somewhere out of sight

The mountain house
incongruous, slap-dab,
reflection in the lake

Through porch spindles—
Purple tulips, white alyssum
line the walk to the raised bridge

North Lookout road—
hawks glide and lift
catching the updrafts

Slap-slap-slap
legs and knees pumping—
paddle boats on the lake

The Traps from Eagle Cliff—
a great whale rises
out of the sea

Fat ice flows
impede our footsteps
in Zaidee's Bower

Going home...
lake porch rocking chairs
filled with melancholy

I LOVE YOUR FACE

(for Jerome)

I love your face
gone from chubby cheek
to thin & whiskered jowl.
From the beginning
the thrill was
to stroke your
silky,
soft,
smooth
baby face.
And now my fingers
reach out
to caress your man face,
and because of love
the thrill isn't less but more.

More Haiku

I glance at my hands
and see oh so many tiny cracks
like crazing on a ceramic bowl

Winter night —
chickadee all puffed up
on my window sill

Bare brown branches
in a water-filled vase —
yellow forsythia!

Hanging flower baskets
swinging gently and dripping—
late Summer rain

Walking sticks
tap, tap, tapping —
blind children cross the bridge

Mary F. Tomaselli

CENTERED ON A RED SPECKLED NOTEBOOK

Since I've been writing poetry,
lines run through my head,
words and phrases,
trying them out,
sometimes, speaking them aloud
to hear the sound.

I go around with a small notebook
and write things down.
Then there are times when
I have to tell myself to stop
and just live life,
instead of seeing how
it's going to look on paper.

PENSEÉS

(for Jerome)

When you're home
you're always there somehow,
on the phone or at my door,
asking questions or helping me
to buy a bookcase for all the books
piled up, this way & that,
on every free space of table & chair.

But when you're in Rhode Island
we hardly ever talk on the phone
and when we do,
your voice is animated, excited,
because you're doing your own thing,
working, learning,
and I miss you terribly.

But last night,
I thought you sounded just a little bit lonely,
missing your family & friends,
and maybe, just maybe,
you were missing me a little too.

PRAYER OF A WOMAN TURNED 50

Please God
don't let me get cancer or a stroke
or a heart attack or some fatal disease,
or hit by a car or a rickshaw,
or get Alzheimer's and go crazy,
just when I'm beginning to find life
so damn interesting.
Amen.

JONES BEACH STORY

The kids sat down next to us
in the sand, speaking English in accents.
it was fuck this and fuck that,
every other word,
except when they stopped
to light cigarettes on matches
behind cupped hands.
I thought:
"Hey, I'll give you my lighter if you can give up
the F-word for 15 minutes,"
but I didn't say it.

I was reluctant to go into the water
and leave my stuff unguarded near them.
Then the clean-cut baby-faced one
asked me to watch *his* stuff—
"My wallet and watch are in these two bags,"
he said, pointing at green & brown backpacks.
"Okaay," I said, "if anybody comes near
I'll give them a mean-looking frown."
And he said, "Just fuckin' punch 'em,"
and I pointed my thumb to the sky and said, "fuckin' A"!

HOTEL CALIFORNIA

Today is Vincent's birthday.
He's in California
in a hotel I failed to get the number of,
so I won't call and sing "happy birthday"
the way I usually do.

Today he's 50, and that's just about the time
people think they're getting old.
Maybe I should put him in touch with
Iris who's just told me there's nothing like
having cancer to start believing in God.

At the bookstore a women's poetry journal pleads for donations:
"Become a matron of the arts."
If there's one thing I don't want to become it's a matron.
Why couldn't it just have said "patron?"

The menu at Ben's is a saga of meat-no-dairy choices:
"Send a salami.
Over 4 lbs. of Hebrew National's old-fashioned best.
Perfect for hanging.
Sent overnight.
$39.95."

At dinner a purple neon drenches our table,
we all look sunburnt.
I tell my mother-in-law that Maria's new boyfriend is a dock worker.
"Oh," she says, "I thought she said doctor."

Vincent calls next evening to thank me
for the salami, and says he's hung it
from the sprinkler spigot
so he can see it from the bed
while he's watching pay-per-view on TV.

HAPPY BIRTHDAY

Play some Debussy for me,
"Afternoon of a Faun,"
or something about Spring or waterfalls.
Please no show tunes.
And don't play "Feelings" under any circumstances,
for God's sake!
Thank you.

Fingers running over the keys,
"Candle in the Wind,"
now I like that one.
A glass of wine,
and no show tunes,
two dollars in the tip glass —
the perfect celebration!

WILLIAM BLAKE KNEW IT

(for Carl)

Grownups are boring.
Somewhere they dropped their sense of humor,
and don't even know it's fallen out of their pockets.

When (I ask you) does it get so sluggish, dull
and plastic?
At what point in Monopoly do you realize
that it's going to be forever Baltic?
At what point do you realize it'll *always* be Trivial Pursuit?
When do you buy that pocket protector,
climb into it, and pull it over your head
so that nothing gets to you,
nothing stings, gooses, or pinches?
When do you make a deal with the angels
that you'll never consort with devils?

The Specialist, or Uphill from Here

We wait on hollow logs
for the pileated woodpecker, subdued for now,
the holes his finished manuscript.
Brandy-tinted leaves interrupt a clear view.
He offers our eyes no mercy,
offers our ears no justice,
And remains hidden.

Mossy Brook

In August,
we put a rock at the confluence of trees
next to the edge of the dry river bed, so that in Spring
we would have a means of measuring the rise of the river
after the thaw.

BOULDER FIELDS

(for Danielle)

Rough paths are primitive paths. Rocks may be wet & slippery. There is danger associated with these paths, with the risk of injury.
They should be attempted only by the agile and experienced hiker with appropriate clothing and footwear.
(from *Hiker's Map of the Mohonk Lake Region)*

Some grow like poppies,
some sit like fat Buddhas
anchored in the earth,
clustered, upended or fallen,
leaning one upon the other.
They offer themselves reluctantly to hand and foot.
We hug them, but we don't love them.
They are strewn along the ridge going south,
schist flashing in the sun.
We move carefully and slowly among them,
hoping for the return of ground flat & unencumbered.

LIVING WILL

Lay me out in sneakers and shorts,
don't spend time looking for a dress.
Give me my hiking stick and
my carabiners with lots of rope.
I want my *Killer Angels* tee-shirt,
and my pillows, but I want the feathers washed and dried first.
Don't bother with my Walkman or *The Crying Game* tape,
I won't need them.
I think I'll need my driver's license,
address book, and photo-gray lenses,
some letters of introduction, and maybe my resume.
Everything else can go to the kids.
and don't forget to notify PBS of my passing,
maybe then they'll stop calling.

THINGS CHANGE

I like change.
I like the unfamiliar.
sameness bores me.
That's why I live where the seasons change,
that's why I don't spend lots of money on clothes or furniture.
Old values are just old,
time-tested ways narrow my options.
That's why I live in the city,
that's why I visit strange places.
What's interesting is what's not like me,
what's entertaining is exotic, alien.
I like eyes that are not round,
skin that is not white, languages I don't understand.
That's why I stay in a place where immigrants settle every day,
that's why I'm not afraid of what this world is coming to.

PINK GRAPE NAIL POLISH

(from a *New York Times* news item, 7/7/95)

The words echo across the river and valley
of the Brazilian rainforest, *"Avon calling!"*
Women in tiny villages sweep shanties
to prepare for her coming.

Today maybe a hot cinnamon lipstick,
or a pink grape nail polish,
or a scented candle to light
the family table at dinner tonight.
The tiny star earrings
may be just the thing
for *festivale* next month.
She'll want a cool drink when she arrives.
It's hot on the river and the path to the village is dry and dusty.
Will she take a chicken in payment today
Or will she insist on gold dust?
She complains when we can't pay
because she has to pay Avon
out of her husband's fishing money.
She says we are lucky to have her
because the river is dangerous,
full of piranhas and poisonous water snakes,
and she could fall in,
just like the Avon lady before her.

THE DONKEYS OF KONA

The sign on Highway 19 says:
"Donkey crossing
next two miles,
dawn & twilight hours."
Curious.

The girl at the Bad Ass Coffee Co.
tells me the donkeys were once used
to haul coffee beans
down the slopes of Mauna Kea,
but now they are wild,
and free to roam the lava fields
to graze on tufts of straw grass,
the only thing that grows there.

She tells me they're in trouble now,
developers want the land
and the donkeys have to go.
Each time we pass that sign I look for them.

And then early one morning
there they are...
five of them, gray & brown,
walking single-file,
heading down to the shore
to spend the day dreaming,
and looking out to the West.

GOOD COMES TO HIM WHO WAITS

There's a gecko under my chair
and he won't come out
so that I can see him.
But I can wait...
I'm in Hawaii and there is
nothing else I have to do.

Mary F. Tomaselli

Christmas Card, 1995

The handsome evergreen
stood alone
reflected in the mirror of the lake.
No one was there
to call it a Christmas Tree.

For Carol

Do you know that Nike commercial?
The one that pictures young girls
saying over and over:
"If you let me play sports, I would
more likely excel in the classroom,
less likely smoke cigarettes & do drugs,
less likely get depressed,
more likely leave a man that beats me,
less likely get breast cancer."

You look wonderful in your uniform
with chest protector & shin guards,
not like a man, but somehow quite feminine.
It could be your blond hair,
but no, that's not it.
To my eyes,
you are comfortable in your clothes,
unisex and square cut,
"no frills" like a generic brand
at the supermarket.
Still there is no mistaking you
for anything but a woman becoming.

Mature Poets Steal

I stole a spool of invisible thread from the 5 & dime
but didn't put it in my pocket.
I held it in my hand right out in the open
and walked out the door.
I was skeptical whether it would work or not.
It was easy to run some onto the sewing bobbin,
but threading the needle was difficult.
Eventually I got the hang of it
and sewed curtains, pillows,
and the rips and tears from all the slings and arrows of my life—
no one was the wiser.

ALLOWANCES

I gave myself permission
to keep a less than perfectly clean house.
I gave myself permission
to think of myself first sometimes.
I gave myself permission
to put my feet up on the couch in the middle of the day.
But I needed Doris Lessing
to give me permission to stop reading a boring book.

FROM A DISTANCE

you don't become a poet
when you're in the middle of it,
nor while you're living through it.
you become a poet after,
when you've been healing for a while,
after, when you're at some distance.
Then you can write about it.

First Born

You've never been able
to admit you're wrong,
the words I'm sorry
stick in your throat.
Twenty nine years, first born
shacked up with first born.
I guess I need less to hear it
than you need not to say it.

FIGHTING
(for Vincent)

We've never really had a good fight,
the way you see them do it on TV
or in the movies:
first you say something, then me, then you...
It always happens like this:
I say something, then I say something else,
and you say nothing, sitting there
in your ugly brown easy chair
with a pained expression...
Then I get crazy and raise my voice,
carrying the argument all by myself,
stomping off, putting lots of dead space between us.
But then all I can see in your face is that familiar expression
and I feel just terrible.

WHEN YOU REMEMBER ME...

(for Audrey)

When you remember me
forget that undertakers painted my face
to quicken me for onlookers;
forget the sightless spasm
that ripped across my brain
and left me with just a fragment of faded genius.
Just remember transitory hyacinths,
clutching horns, unredeemable desire,
dropping-down pleasures,
and the rare hysterical kyrie
of the doves.

The Coming of Age

I bless you, old man,
disoriented, looking behind at cars.
I'm there with you.
Get home on wobbly legs,
alone, plastic bag of groceries
pulling at your red, arthritic fingers.
I'll hold you up in my mind
so you'll move along sure-footed
over sidewalk & asphalt.
I know I'll be you someday not far off,
hoping someone, not yet so old,
will see me
and bless me
against the coming of age.

FORTUNE COOKIES (I)

We had Chinese food last night.
I threw away those little packets of soy sauce and duck sauce,
and the hard little cookies with the fortunes inside.
I'm not superstitious, but I couldn't stop thinking
about them.
At midnight I got up and went downstairs
to retrieve those cookies
and here is what they said:
"You will read a book by Barbara Taylor Bradford,"
"You will successfully give up smoking this year,"
"You will attend your first healing Mass,"
"You will finish all those needlepoint pictures you've started."
Baloney!
I shut the light and went back to bed.

ASH WEDNESDAY

The girl at the nail salon asked,
what's that smudge there?
The lady with gray hair getting the cheap manicure
raised her hand to her forehead
and touched it gently with one stripped and filed finger.
Oh it's ashes...
"Uh-huh," said the girl.

I know what's behind putting that sooty stain
right out there, like a beacon—
this is not the time to talk of pearly gates
and that invisible something that lives forever.
Those splotches of burnt palm say:
you are nothing more than dust,
so don't think you're hot shit or anything
and (as if that weren't enough)
you're not going anywhere but into the ground
where you'll join all that other biodegradable stuff
you've been so careful to use for washing dishes and clothes.

There, that should knock a little humility into you.

It's All about Food

My mother gave up cooking when my father died.
She was never any good at it anyway.
Her specialty was Spanish Franks:
canned sauce, red and glutinous,
frankfurters cut in chunks.
I didn't think she hated cooking,
it was just that she was of the "eat-to-live"
not the "live-to-eat" school.
Dinners were colorless and spare,
her worst fear was leftovers.
She believed she made just enough—
it was usually not enough.

My father kept a Goodie Closet,
chock full of candy bars, big ones.
Mr. Goodbar was his favorite.
I took to stealing from it,
breaking off pieces carefully,
not to give myself away.

Some people say the care and attention
a woman gives to the preparation of food
is an expression of the depth of her love...
there's a lesson in there somewhere.

DIANA

She stood on the threshold
like a huntress,
like one of Albee's fierce destroyers,
blood dripping from her teeth,
(it seemed)
a devouring coyote.
She made no pretense.
Hollow moonlight drenched her shoulders,
indissoluble light consecrated her progress,
generous and unnatural.
Spanish eyes sparked
and interrupted the surging clamor,
voices suppressed waited
while she flung the necklace from her.
White, rounded pieces of offal
rolled to his feet.
He was shocked to the marrow.

MATISSE'S GOLDFISH

(for the man in the hospital bed)

They're moving me to isolation tonight.
The guy in the neat white coat
with red ribbon on the collar says,
something's just not right.
They wanted me on a gurney,
but I asked to go by wheelchair,
sitting up, dragging my tubes behind me.
Masks & gloves from now on.
They'll have to test my wife & kids
if the culture grows up to be TB or something nastier.
Hospital green single room with double doors and no knobs,
leave everything in the vestibule coming in, going out,
no ice cubes from the pantry anymore,
they'll bring them in sterile plastic bag.
But Matisse's Goldfish are on the wall in front of me.
looking peaceful in a jar on a pinkish table—
I think I want to join them for a swim.

SHE TOLD ME ONCE

(for Carl)

when she is dying,
she wants to see
(if she can see)
the face of her nephew
there at the side of the bed.
That it is because of him
she stands a chance of getting into heaven
(if there is a heaven).
It is because of him
she won't have to make amends,
do penance, seek redemption,
or wait for the blessings of a priest.
It is because of him
that she caught a glimpse
of what it's like to have a child
and love him.

KUWAITI CAMEL

(based on a Reuter's report)

You went missing
after the Iraqi occupation
5 years ago.
You had gotten lost amid the flames
and smoke that settled
on the hot dry desert
after the Storm.
The miracle was that you weren't killed,
and found your way back,
after all this time,
to Mohammed al-Auwaisheer,
who wrote a poem
(in his happiness)
praising your loyalty.
You were in perfectly good health,
but Mohammed was surprised
when he found out you were pregnant.

Poem

Did she say Zantac or Zanax?
Damn, it matters, it does!
For heartburn's not
the same as panic.
One is a trifle and will not turn
the heart to ashes,
just a backup, like traffic on
the bridge on Friday afternoon.
But the other is black,
blue swirls on synapses,
dropping down on the chest
like a fat odalisque—
I wouldn't want to waste my sympathy.

FORTUNE COOKIES (II)

Do you remember we used to read
those little fortunes curled into folded cookies,
folded inside those curled & crackly cookies?
We used to read them greedily
when we were young,
when possibilities were as limitless & bright
as poppies in a field,
when it all lay before us
and nothing was behind.
But this morning, three little papers
lay on the table,
the bits of hard, tanned dough long since eaten.
Did you read them?
And if you did, why didn't you tell me?

PAUL OF TARSUS

Some scholars say Jesus
had no intention,
never had any intention
of founding a new religion.
Paul was the one
who turned the Jews away.
Paul was the one who said,
Jesus was God—
Jesus was Messiah—
the New Testament replaces the Old—
And these things stuck in the throat of Jews like a fishbone.
Jesus had no intention
of founding a new religion,
He never had any intention.

At the Lake

It's been a long time since I've seen so many white faces gathered together in one place. Pale, pale skins turning red in the hot sun. This place is just two hours from the city by car; not a long way to go to find so much homogenized sameness.

The only yellow I see are the tops of small beach umbrellas. The only brown I see are some old leaves gathered in drains near the concession stand.

I've lived a long time in the city, and when my people gather at the beach, park or concert, we are a colorful bunch: a display as diverse & lovely as a summer garden, like a multi-colored crazy quilt, like handfuls and handfuls of confetti flung across the grass.

The Nose

(for my mother)

My face is the face
of the woman who bore me.
The eyes, dark and opaque like hers,
the mouth, not as thin-lipped,
but still reminiscent.
And the nose, ah yes, the nose.
Unlike her, I don't hide it with laced handkerchief.
I'm not ashamed as she was all her life.
The nose of her father and her father's father,
that she might have been proud of.

We Used to Complain

about the petty responsibilities
and great expectations:
milking cows,
doing wash,
balancing checkbooks,
beating rugs,
paying bills,
drawing water,
birthing children,
kissing boo-boos,
washing dishes,
washing diapers,
washing windows,
answering the phone,
answering questions,
wiping away tears,
wiping behinds,
changing batteries,
sweeping floors,
gathering eggs,
ironing clothes,
making beds,
making appointments,
making meals,
cutting coupons,
keeping peace,
rendering fat,
watering horses,
celebrating birthdays,
checking homework,
churning butter,
rewinding videotapes,
feeding the dog,

feeding the cat,
combing hair,
cleaning the car,
cleaning the toilet,
bolstering egos,
opening mail,
tending the sick
waking the dead.

But when there is a poem on a page
that needs finishing, a story that needs revising,
a canvas that needs filling, an instrument or a book waiting,
then we shut up and put up with anything.

Fish Oil Capsules

Take vitamin E in the morning,
they say it will keep you from
heart attack or stroke
from smoking or eating the wrong things.
Garlic tablets, too,
and fish oil capsules.
So I take one or the other every day
to guard against the inevitable.
I wonder, if I take all three,
will I live forever?

PENNIES & BOOK MATCHES

Pennies weigh me down.
I accumulate them
like dust beneath my bed.
They're hardly worth the trouble
of picking up except
if you drop one in the house...
a penny does a lot of damage
to a good vacuum cleaner.
I accumulate book matches, too.
Not the kind you keep in a glass bowl
on the coffee table to show everyone
the fancy restaurants you've been to,
just the plain ones that pile up in the kitchen drawer
which won't close unless you squash them down
with one hand and shove with the other.
I guess we can all live without pennies...
but what do you do with a cigarette
when you can't find your lighter?

MAJOR APPLIANCES

I'm shooting my major appliances today,
they're about to be repossessed.
I wouldn't want to be taken
forcibly from my home,
unless I was going to a sandy beach
where guys in bikinis
were serving Rum Bushwackers.
If I let them live they'll go to
a junk yard or be auctioned off
to the highest bidder.
They'll have to go home
with who-knows-what sort of person.
I'll do it quickly and humanely
making sure I get them right between the eyes.
I'll have none linger.
They won't know what hit them,
I'm sure they'll be grateful.

Blue Ceramic Teapot

(for Audrey)

I lifted the teapot
from its place on the shelf,
one of many full of kitchen things.
I was browsing when my eye caught it
and I thought of you:
dying there in your bed,
crying sometimes,
saying, with your daughters' help,
the last things that need saying.
And I thought of all the days we had spent together
and felt the terrible distance between us,
me holding a little blue ceramic teapot
and you there in your bed dying.
I hoped you could feel my mind full of you.

TOUGH LIFE

The conversation in the back seat
  went like this:
"I don't ever want to go McDonald's ball room again."
"Why?"
"People throw up in there!"
"Yeah, Discovery Zone is puke city!"
"Yeah, puke everywhere!"...

And you thought kids had it easy.

Mary F. Tomaselli

FIDEL IN NEW YORK

(from a news story, 1995)

Castro says he's not voting for Giuliani
in the next election
because of potholes in the streets,
the construction, the graffiti,
plastic bags hanging from trees,
and the noise...

On his island they're selling
pizzas with melted condoms on top,
cutting up rag mops and eggs for sandwiches,
paying a month's salary for the taste of an apple,
taking baths with leaves because there is no soap.
There's no milk or medicines for babies,
no work for the fathers,
no books, paper or pencils for schoolchildren...

He should talk.

My Blue Feet

My blue feet
stuffed into little red shoes
(you know the kind the Pope wears?)
ache for yellow hair
and a baby face.
But my heart is black
and my years are long & graying.
Bright white philosophers have nothing for me,
I've danced the fast dances long enough,
the end is closer than I think.

Almost Perfect

Lilacs appeared on a gray day
burdened with rain
and bent,
brushing the walk with purple lips.
Leaves coming green
in spite of the chill,
the wet and the wind.
I brought the cluster to my nose,
anticipating the sweet, familiar scent,
but there was none.

Returning

The swallows are going—
lucky birds!
They take with them a new moon,
a new forest, a new thought—
Capistrano is not for me.

INHALING A FANTASY

(for Carl)

I smoked pot with the kid
who's had my heart for 20 years.
"Auntie" he said,
do you want to share a toke with me,
since you've never done it,
and I've come into some quite suddenly?"
And the offer sucked the heart and brain out of me.
The park turned green, breeze after breeze
and we two, we two, breathed into each other's
eyes and soul.
And I, I stopped listening to angry voices
that topped the trees,
and inhaled the sweetness.

Monday Morning

She was sitting at the kitchen table
when the TV said,
Shock therapy is back in vogue
for treating depression.
He said,
Oh, then maybe you should
get to some of the electrical work
that needs doing around here.
She put her head down on the table
and laughed out loud.

English Movies, English Tea

(for Audrey)

I bet she misses short stories,
(especially William Trevor's)
hanging flower baskets,
new lipsticks,
talking to Richard,
polishing brass,
English movies,
English tea,
discussing novels,
snuggling with Suki,
art galleries,
her children,
her grandson.
I bet she misses us—
just like we miss her.

Life Ever After

Unholy flames singe the mahogany
and crumple the wildflowers
resting there.
Flames not meant to purify,
(there's nothing to make clean)
but to obliterate,
so no one will have to spend
the anniversary standing
over grassy plots, mumbling,
while kids run in and out
of stones leaving blobs of bubble gum
to show someone's been there.

It was once believed that consignment
to flames denied the promise:
the reunion of body & soul at the end of it all
(no one wondered how they'd find each other).
But now it's too crowded
and expedient to burn bodies,
I guess the souls will just have to spend eternity alone.

LUCK & THE TRUE CROSS

I found out today
that when you "knock wood"
you're calling on the power
of Christ's cross to ward off
the bad things.
I told my Jewish friend
and he stopped knocking.
He was upset, though,
that he was without a quick fix
for evil.
He tried knocking on aluminum
and plastic, but it never felt right.
so he went back to knocking on wood—
he's the luckiest guy I know.

THURSDAY MORNING

We were at the beach
catching rays,
as they say.
Me, drinking coffee,
milk, two sugars,
he, slugging Diet Pepsi,
his mouth on the dirty lid.
We lit cigarettes with cupped hands.
The two of us sitting, sunning, smoking
in the biggest, fucking ash tray in the world.

ON THE EDGE

I
I wish I could pull my ear
like Carol Burnett
to let everyone watching know
I'm okay—
even when I'm not.

II
Nothing had better happen now.
My mother better not die, or
have a stroke, or my friend's plans
for the new house fall through.
And he better not test positive,
or she have cancer again.
Because right now it's all I can do
to make it through the ordinary days.

MAN OF GOD

He called himself a man of God, but couldn't stand living upstairs from the lesbian couple who were his landlords. He called them "lesboes" and hunted places in the Bible where what he imagined they did together was condemned. Sometimes early Sunday morning, on his way to services, he'd pass them making love in their car in the driveway. It sickened him.

He was an Elder of the church, elected for his Christian charity & prayerfulness, but when he'd pass their door at night, he'd curse them, and wish down fire & brimstone upon them. He told his kids to stay away and not talk to them.

When he had the opportunity, he moved without notice and demanded his security with interest which the couple didn't have. When he threatened lawyer & small claims court, they told him to come back Monday night. He stopped the new tenants in the street and poisoned their opinion.

On Monday evening, he left a Little League game to collect his money. When the lesbians opened the door, they shot him in the head with a .44. The new tenants helped bury the body in the backyard and deflect questions asked by detectives the next day.

Snow

Like a cold blanket,
an arctic shroud, white,
like Christ's draped from the Easter cross.
Redemptive and pristine,
an almost welcome cover-up.
Clay for mitten sculptures,
like a new infant's soul,
a momentary treat,
warm tongues catching flakes through chattering teeth.

Reading Seamus Heaney, Poet

Turkeys plucked, and tadpoles,
old women in church, and father
digging potatoes.
I can hear the brogue,
a lilt in the voice,
but there's no laughter there.
There's a wistfulness, a sadness
in the white spaces,
that they say is deep in the psyche
of those of us who come from there,
that green and troubled island.

Prose Poems

Vacation

A place to bring a chair, and a book, where necessary voices are muted. It may be ocean, lake, or ski slope, for the purpose of recess and vacancy. Shaded eyes in a head dropping back, with breath emitted slowly, languorously. Or watching a fading hawk, hanging below the ridge, during a rest-stop and a cup of water. It's a place for lying down, or leaning forward on oars for a time. To some, as unnecessary and wasteful as a rose bouquet.

Library

Solid, concrete and low-slung, like the people who man the shelves. You may think a whole world opens up with the door. But it's only some parts. Classified, arranged, accommodating a universe. Solitary, silent members with a whole lot to say if only they were encouraged. They are lettered and well-informed, but lack the glitz and ease of modern technologies. Frequented by children and old people.

Church

A white spire is noticeable in the landscape from any distance. A house of immateriality casting shadows through stained glass and baptismal water. Shades of saintliness to look up to; it's all anathema to familiar spirits and their familiars. Years of incense and orthodoxy permeate wood and alabaster. The drama unfolding center stage is neither comedy nor tragedy. It is the place where the Promise is reiterated to the disillusioned.

Nursing Home

Roaming pale dried-out wraiths on highly-polished linoleum, in and out, in terry robes washed and dried many times. Rooms off corridors, unlocked doors, a cactus never dies from lack of water. The vacant face at the window doesn't recognize the face at the door, but smiles anyway. The community room is lit by a muted TV and the voice of the Arts & Crafts lady shows everyone how to cut paper. At 4 o'clock, they wait for little white cups.

Mary F. Tomaselli

MONTAUK VACATION

What I wanted to do was take a shower,
open a bottle of cheap wine
and watch the forties flick
on Channel 5—
detective played by Mickey Spillane
(he should have stuck to writing).
The place was all scrub pine
and cheap modern decor.

I opened the '79 Chateau Laurette
not cheap by any stretch.
it was smooth and mellow,
the color of urine,
but that didn't put me off.

I felt rich and lucky,
Georgia O'Keefe's ubiquitous red poppy
was on the wall.
I didn't mind,
it was enough to evoke my feminine side.

Earlier that week I visited
Mr. Koppelman's nature preserve
and walked the cliffs above the Sound,
on the only afternoon it hadn't rained.

COMINGS & GOINGS

He lies there dying
in the room above the windows.
They come and go
and park their cars along the grass & gravel.
His brother takes the little girl
who seems not to know.
They walk and sometimes she runs,
he guards against her falling.
Cars gather and then they're gone.
This is the vigil
and we've been watching for days.
Time, for us, is marked by the comings and goings.
Does he mark time?
By the shaft of light along the length of shade,
by murmurings outside the door,
by the figure in white above the bed,
by the comings and goings of faces
he used to know and still loves?
When I used to speak to him at the fence,
gray face, baggy pants,
he would tell me that the crocuses had bloomed
in the front yard or that his little girl
had called him "Daddy."
Is the drama any greater now that
he's there in the room above the windows
while I keep watch in the dimming light?

Mary F. Tomaselli

STEINBECK'S *EAST OF EDEN*

He writes his story
of Cain & Abel,
no mere copy and simple reiteration.
He writes on the *recto*,
too difficult to write on the left,
right, left: two sides of the brain,
two sides of the body,
two places on either side of the throne of God.
He makes a callus
(on the 3rd finger of his writing hand)
sometimes rough & raw,
sometimes tight and shiny.
His callus is on the right,
mine is on the left,
right, left, like the two brothers
in the story.
It is his retelling of one of the two oldest stories
in the world:
the one about free will and guilt and forgiveness.
It is his "big book," his "long book."
He worries about pencils,
they must be long
(he gives them away when they grow short)
and sharp and plentiful.

And so there are choices,
and we have made them,
you & I,
not so much wrong ones or right ones,
but, maybe, wise and wiser—
we have been brothers from the beginning.
I'd gladly be Cain to your Abel
if I could keep you from the cancer
and regret,
I'd give you Eden if I could,
and gladly wander the rest of my days for the giving.

WAITING FOR THE POET

In the first full moon
the boy stood
waiting for the poet
to finish her poem.
The poem was for him,
using the word
he had given her.
I watched the boy
in the moonlight,
the beautiful boy,
who could have been my lover.

NOTES FROM MOHONK

We can't imagine the Festival of the Arts
without an appearance by tap dancing great,
Brenda Buffalino.

Soft slap-slap-slapping of my slip-ons echoing through the halls.

We thought of stealing towels—
how big a sin could it be?
They're not even 100% cotton!

The names of two flowers in the formal gardens,
Evolvulus and Penisedum.
We agree there is something vaguely erotic about them.

Ron says Vinny's going to put my ashes in a music box
and every time you open the lid it'll play, "Smoke Gets in Your Eyes."

Back from Bonticou Crag
exhausted from a 7 mile hike
the van driver asks for our passes,
and we say, "We don't need no stinkin' passes, just let us on the van."

And the ugly pigeon-toed lady checks the daily activities at the front desk.

Poem Dying

As in the departure of the soul,
or Horace Greeley's imperative,
as words do on the tongue,
sworn to by shades or spooks of past lives,
like dust and ashes,
or the remains of the day,
dusk and also winter.
Referred to when caught red-handed,
betrayed by blood pools after a massacre,
often accompanied by dirge or elegy,
muffled drum, or procession,
shocking in the high drama of hara-kiri,
or the petty violence of muzzle to temple.
The goal of martyrs and saints,
hunters and hounds,
more fun when it's about ties and tee-shirts.

Dress casual

I want a job in talk radio
so I don't have to put on make-up
in the mornings.
It's odd to see Susan Hayward
in evening gowns in the middle of the day.
White gloves went out just after I started
teaching high school,
men haven't had to wear jackets
in restaurants for years,
"No Bare Feet" says it all these days.
I wear the same earrings 'til I buy a new pair.
Does anyone buy an Easter outfit anymore?
At the clothes store you can't tell the little girl things
from the little boy things.
I have one pair of "dress-up" shoes for funerals and the like,
and three pairs of sneakers: knock-around,
everyday, and "good."

AUTUMNAL EQUINOX

I can hear the traffic
through my window
and the distant rumble of planes.
I can see the houses close together,
black-topped driveways,
straggly potted geraniums still swinging
over doorways.
The maple leaves are fading, as expected.
The sky is in the process of darkening
as I write to commemorate this day
when light equals darkness.
I feel an intermittent breeze,
chilly, no longer warm,
that makes me think of sweaters and socks,
galoshes and snow.
I will close the window now
to begin the waiting.

(written for Project Equinox 1996)

In Other (British) Words...

Is a police line-up an identity parade?
Or the trunk of a car a boot?
If you looked in your boot would you find
a dead body or a jack to fix a flat?
And what could you fix with a jack in a flat in Soho?
You'd be happy if you weighed 9 stone,
but do you know how much 9 stones weigh?
Do you think a barman is as gentle as a bartender?
We may drink but do we do as Lords do?
If we needed a lift would we expect an elevator?
Certainly we'd rather a letter miscarry
than a woman three months pregnant.
Wouldn't we be at sixes and sevens,
if they put us in jail for cooking the books.
What would you do with a
limb of the law,
bad lot,
ship turned turtle,
sheet anchor,
not half hot cup of coffee?
Oh, bloody hell, pass the milk and sugar.

Mary F. Tomaselli

SMALL REMINDERS

(for Jimmy)

They took the old piano today,
wrapped so carefully in a blanket,
like a big black baby going on a journey.
Upended on a dolly,
it slid easily down the walk to the curb.
I watched from the door
as they strained and lifted it aboard the yellow van,
and strapped it down as you might
an obstreperous mental patient.

I kneel on the floor in the room
where the piano once stood,
there's a faint scent of wood like eucalyptus.
I rub the places where the carpet was crushed
by the weight of it,
but the nap won't be coaxed,
dark impressions remain -
small reminders.

NO UNAUTHORIZED DUMPING

She said:
Don't tell me your sad story
unless you want to sit through mine.
I assure you mine's sadder.
Don't corner me with ghastly details
of surgeries and accidents,
I can no longer commiserate
with "ums" and "ahs,"
brief comforting expressions.
Don't remove the bandage
to show me your latest wound,
my imagination can picture the unimaginable.
Don't assume I will be surprised
by what it is your children do—
children have been doing so for centuries.
Assume all that is human has been
experienced before, done before,
expressed before in enough clichés
to fill a packing box.
And then, in the silence that follows,
consider the clear, the interesting,
the succinct, the unadorned...

And for God's sake, keep this in mind
when you're writing a poem!

READING HABITS

Kurt Vonnegut rode to the shopping center
yesterday on the roof of her car.
how he got there is another story.
It wasn't the first time an author had made the trip:
John Updike, F. Scott Fitzgerald,
and 50 New American Poets had done it too.
It wasn't that she *made* them ride up there,
she just hadn't realized it.
If she had, she would've had them ride in the passenger seat
wearing their seat belts, of course.
How they stayed up there was nothing to marvel at,
she was a careful driver, always had been.
She was proud to say she'd never had an accident
(knock wood!)
and drove defensively on most occasions.
It wasn't just authors that rode on the roof of her car—
once a bag of groceries made it from Waldbaum's on 20th Avenue
to her house on 14th,
intact and standing upright.
What amazed her was that no one noticed
Kurt or the poets sitting up there,
at least, no one ever motioned to her,
pointing over her head, as far as she could remember.
It's a shame, she thought,
people just don't read much anymore.

CHRISTMAS IN TUZLA (1995)

The reports say they're
young and scared.
The Army plays bloody videos
to get them in the mood.
They've packed away all their belongings
in a big warehouse 'till their return.
There's a Christmas tree on the tarmac
decorated with cards from a Girl Scout troop
and a priest says Mass in a field cleared of mines.
They're feeling all cozy and patriotic
because they've been told they're here to save lives
and keep the peace.
The radio announces the first casualty
who'll receive a Purple Heart for his bloodied leg,
blown up when he hit a mine in a field they forgot to clear.
He's lucky, they'll be sending him home in time for New Year's.

Mary F. Tomaselli

Faces Barbados

In Bridgetown
I swim in a sea of black faces
and wonder who they think I am
if they think of me at all.

Why do I expect a smile
on all the faces on the bus,
acknowledgement, acceptance
of me,
an obvious interloper?

Singled out
by the shop owner
he beckons me to the front of the line,
his arm making a sweeping arc,
as if to say
"No white face waits in my shop!"
I should have objected
and stood my ground
but I didn't.

He acknowledges me
with a "thumbs up"
and a smile when I order
jerk chicken and salad.
The smile on his face
is genuine, I want to believe,
making him appear younger
than he must be.

Who lives in those pretty houses
behind solid white walls?
I'm afraid I know…
Who lives in those tin-roofed shacks
behind rusting, rotting autos
growing in front yards?
I'm afraid I know…
Ought we depend on their being satisfied
with their lot?
I think not.

GETTING TO MIDNIGHT

It's 10 o'clock on New Year's Eve,
oh God, it feels like twelve.
Let's get to the damn ball and countdown,
the kissing and wishing everyone Happy New Year
so I can go home to bed.
The same cast of characters every year,
but tonight Clarissa's come, the manic-depressive in-law,
who went after her husband with a kitchen knife
and spent time in the cuckoo ward
(I thought at the time she had never been more sane).
She's pinned me against the stove
where the sixth tray of something stuffed, rolled, or sliced,
is beginning to burn,
and she's telling me about her neighbor,
the 76-year-old doctor, who everyone thinks is her lover.
"I wanted to invite him tonight but the hostess nixed it."
Clarissa's pissed. She says he's been impotent for 10 years,
only takes her to the opera and Broadway shows.
What I notice is nobody's rescuing me,
and my ass is beginning to burn along with the hors d'oeuvres...
and it's still an hour to midnight.

DRIVING

Just finished that book where
the 40-year-old housewife walks out
because her husband doesn't care
and the children don't appreciate her.
Not me—
When I feel like that
I just get in my car and drive,
shove Rod Stewart or Aerosmith
into the dashboard and turn it up LOUD.
I press my arms against the steering wheel,
my back into the seat,
striking my heel on the floor
in time with the strong, hard beat.
'Til I'm somewhere or nowhere,
cruising to the words of "Hot Legs," or "Love in an Elevator,"
not giving a damn whether anyone appreciates me or not.

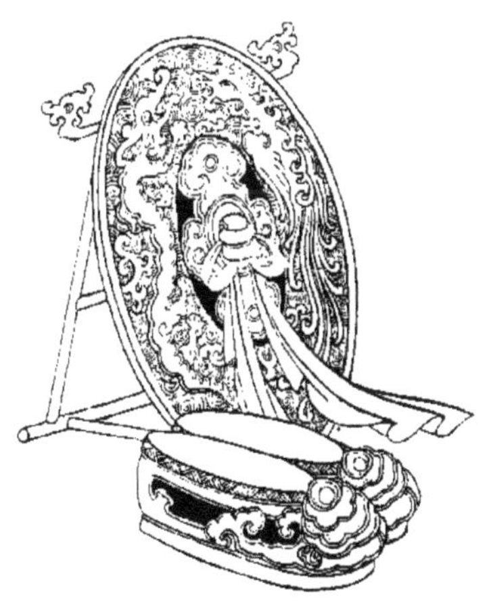

Rules for the Snow

(from a news item, 1/25/96)

Don't throw snowballs in Flushing,
don't throw snowballs in Queens,
because if you get drunk
and throw snowballs, it seems
people don't like it,
and you'll end up lying in the snow
with a bullet in your neck.

CONVERSATION

Outside the bookstore 4-year-old Chelsea said:
    Mom, that girl was being bad, wasn't she?
Mom said:
    Yes, but I know another little girl who does the same thing, don't I?
Chelsea said (exasperated):
    But Mom, I'm a new tree!
Mom is puzzled for a moment and then it dawns:
    Do you mean you're turning over a new leaf?
Chelsea beamed:
    Exac'ly.

Mary F. Tomaselli

Love Poem

I saw a pair of fat red lips
on the marble floor
and, though your lips
were never red like those,
or as voluptuous,
I thought of you.
It may have been that
you were already there
somewhere in the back of my mind
waiting to be thought about.

You, who used to call me
and make me think you needed me.
You, who let me in on all your little secrets,
ones you said you never told anyone else,
you who weren't quite lying.

You see I had never felt so preferred,
so elected by another to serve with such purpose.
And you *were* needy.
I don't know who you talk to now,
or, maybe, you've grown
to keep your own counsel...

the lips on the floor were as silent
as you are on the subject.

30 YEARS MARRIED

I go about and read my books
and write my poems
and they congratulate me,
lighting candles, marking the occasion.
30 years married,
a very long time for a marriage
or a war.

I suppose there was a sense of direction,
in the beginning,
or maybe it was luck,
or an angel.

Easy promises made
to love & honor,
easy because we were so young,
and there was nothing to lose, I suppose,
and the commitment was agreed to
without hesitation
or reflection.

And yet they marvel,
while I don't know what it is
I've done to merit the celebration.

I can offer no answer,
no advice
to those who want to know the secret,
who are sure there *is* a secret.
I go about and read my books
and write my poems
and say:
                                        Once
I was young,
and now I'm 30 years married.

Gandhi

They're throwing marigolds and rose petals
on the coffin containing my ashes.
They're chanting my name, hip deep
in the holy waters of the Ganges and Yamuna.
These ashes, my own ashes,
have lain all these years in the dark,
in a vault, cold and gray, forgotten.

I walked the earth with these people once
and stood on the riverbank with them,
loved them and died for them.
Holy men wrap themselves in saffron,
women rest on a sandbar,
in this country, where some now call me
enemy.

Give me back my ashes!
Toss them to the wind!
Let them sink below the surface of your memory
and become one with my soul
which runs down to the sea.

NO DREAM OF GARDENS

I have no dream of gardens,
luscious and green,
like the Daintree rainforest
I once knew.
No dream of blue-green water,
diamond-flashing palm tree
black against the sun.
No dream of a place to go
when it's over,
and I'm shut up in a drawer
in a wall of drawers.
No dream of a beatific face, welcoming,
at the bright end of a darkened hallway.
No dream of forever, ever after
after life, except
that someone might remember.

FEBRUARY

I brought home the sun
from the tropical island
and laid it on my bed,
smoothing it out to the edges.
It shone bright and warmed the wintry room.
When tropical flowers grew there,
and filled the room with scent and color,
I thought it would be enough ‘til Spring.

St. Martin, FWI

I answered you when you called
and sat before you Buddha-like,
leaning back against your legs,
facing away, looking out on the lagoon.
Your fingers worked quickly,
strand after strand,
squeezing little bits of foil,
threading beads two at a time.

You spoke in an island melody,
expressing breeze and heat.
I thought you might tell me a story
of Africa, or the Arawak.
Lifting my face to the Caribbean sun
I dreamed this was my island
and not yours.

On My Way Out

I've made it a rule of my life
never to leave the house for anything
but the joyous.
Don't ask me to put in an appearance,
or pick you up from the station,
or drive you to an appointment,
or attend another fundraiser,
show up for dinner at your mother's.
I'm on my way out
to pick up pizza and a good movie.

UNCONDITIONAL

(for Carl)

It used to be
we'd shop the mall together,
pouring over cheap videos,
searching shelves for sci-fi books,
Nivens & Pournelle's.
Once we saw two guys run
for the exit doors of parking level one,
and when they passed around coupons
for free McDLT's we took two each,
then gave them to the bag lady
dragging all her goods behind her.
I'd buy you a present
and you'd buy me one.
you wouldn't mind eating lunch
in the smoking section,
and that's when I'd tell you
I'd always love you no matter what.

JOURNEYS

It was a long time in the coming,
arrival was a far way.
But I made the journey in early Spring
to continue another begun some 30 years ago.

It was the daffodils and forsythia that drew me on,
reservoirs, bright and full, a pond,
a barn standing there for 200 years.
How did I know a pheasant would cross the river to show itself to me?
The sing-song of an absent bird
(a mockingbird, I think) was my only greeting.
Until you, dear guide and companion appeared on the step,
and I knew I had arrived at the place you described.

It was an earthly place, meant for horses, you said.
But the swing set, set apart, told me it was your home.
Your move had worried me,
left me wondering if I'd have to go it alone,
but you were reassuring,
sitting there in that bright and graceful room…
May I use those trees to mark the seasons by?

RITE OF BAPTISM OF A CHILD

I reach out to anyone
who will pick me up and take me in their arms.
I don't speak,
but cry out in short sharp screams.
At two, I'm very small and fragile,
With blue, papery skin.
My face has a foreign look.
My new mother has dressed me all in white,
put a wreath of small white blossoms in my hair,
hair that's flat and thin at the back
from lying long hours in a cot in a Moscow orphanage.

Sometimes I begin to rock,
in the middle of everything
I smile a crooked smile for the photographer,
everyone is amazed that I stand so still,
staring into the eye of the camera.

This is the ceremony
that casts out devils, they tell me,
and makes my new name official.
My old one has been banished,
I'll never hear it spoken again.
My new mother believes
I'm beginning to understand some English
(it's not true).

I don't look around for my new mother,
I don't settle into anyone's arms,
until the music plays and I fall asleep exhausted,
to dream a dream of something,
anything, familiar.

CREMATION

(for Vincent)

What will it be like
when you are gone and I am left behind?
No socks on the radiator
warming, waiting for your feet,
feet never to be warm again.
No sound of your voice, just dead silence.
I'll have to keep the radio on
to stop the awful stillness from pressing in.
The empty wing chair will feel the chilliness
And want to fly away to embrace some other body still warm.
And the bed — Ah, yes, the bed, too, will feel your absence.
(It's difficult to speak of frigid sheets!)
But the worst will be the knowledge
that you have been left alone, out there,
cold, among silent stones and strangers
who will not greet you warmly,
or make you feel at home.
And I will regret I didn't stand my ground
and let the fiery blaze turn you to a precious dust
for me to keep nearby upon my homey hearth.

GRANDMA

Her face in the window of the big gray house
watching me every day cross the lots to school,
rhubarb grew in her yard
and I'd watch her cut it up to make pies.
I loved best the heart cookies made just for me
from leftover dough: sprinkled with
sugar, thin, crispy, melting on the tongue,
she'd wave from that window and smile.
My brother and I were sent to the playground
across the boulevard the day grandfather died
in his bed set up in the piano room.
She gave up the house after that
and moved in with her sister at the back of a delicatessen.

She always seemed old and frail to me,
snow white hair held in a net,
thin, skin bluish, transparent.
She'd had the mastoid bone
behind her right ear operated on years ago
and the deep crevice there caught my eye
when she turned her head.
She smelled like Lilies of the Valley.
and wore a small diamond-studded ring on a bony, arthritic finger.

She said, I want you to have it someday.
She fingered rosary beads when she sat in the parlor,
a small prayer book filled with holy cards lay on her lap.
She never spoke about her husband but I know
she prayed for him— he needed the prayers, she said,
he was Episcopalian, and she wasn't sure he could get into heaven on his own.
Some afternoons I'd visit, and we'd watch the soaps.
When she died, she died alone,
sitting in a wing-backed chair in her bedroom,
I wish I could have been there.

Mary F. Tomaselli

Going to the Movies

I opened the sunroof and side window,
threw my coat in the backseat,
and drove to the movie house,
but when I got there I couldn't go in.
There were two movies I wanted to see,
my afternoon was free,
but I couldn't go in.
I sat in the car
watching others buying tickets,
checking my watch,
half listening to noon-hour talk radio.
When it was too late,
I drove to the grocer's
and picked up frozen fish for dinner,
there was no fresh bread.
I drove to the promenade
along the edge of the Bay
and watched the men putting their boats
in the water.
The sun went in and it grew cold.
I drove to the bookstore
(I had a list in my pocket),
but the shelves were empty,
or so it seemed to me.

SOUVENIRS

(for Grace)

Were you hurt
when we gave back
the perfume you brought us
from the islands?
Were you? When she said,
not my scent, and I pleaded allergies?
You were unruffled and
apologized for the mistake.
Would anyone else have reacted with such aplomb?

PLANE CRASH

...and a pandemonium of women & children,
debris on a sea like an envelope, and dark.
There are limbs, big & small, riding
the crests of waves.
A certain whirring comes & goes
with rescue on its mind,
afraid that the job is not rescue,
only the collection of parts,
delivery for identification.
Families phone dentists for the charts.
Making piles in temporary morgues,
making mountains on reluctant shores,
it is the business of cleaning-up
that horrifies us.

ABOUT THE AUTHOR

Mary F. Tomaselli teaches literature and memoir writing in the Continuing Education Department of Queensborough Community College in Bayside, NY. Her poems (some of which are included here) have been published in such journals as *Savannah Literary Journal, The Muddy River Poetry Review, Arrowsmith, Poetry in Motion, Brussels Sprout, Poetry Motel, and Coffeehouse Magazine.* Ms. Tomaselli has her master's degree in Library and Information Science from Queens College of the City University of New York and has worked as an indexer and library consultant for 25 years. She's a person who believes that to live to be 100 (she's more than half way there!) you need to drink lots of cafeinated coffee and learn to put the toilet paper roll on the right way (not backwards!) She's entirely grateful that her husband, Vincent, never held her to the promise that she would live in a cold-water flat with him when they were married 34 years ago.

www.ingramcontent.com/pod-product-compliance
Ingram Content Group UK Ltd.
Pitfield, Milton Keynes, MK11 3LW, UK
UKHW040016200726
13854UKWH00001B/225

9 780759 632158